Enter here!

This year you
worlds of FLU

MW01705168

You will learn how to write faster using special joins.

You will develop a writing style that is easily read by others.

JOB APPLICATION: HANDWRITING EXPLORER

Name: ______________________________

Date of birth: ______________________________

Previous handwriting experience: ______________________________

____

____

Why I would make a good handwriting explorer: ______________________________

____

____

APPLICATION SUCCESSFUL

YOU MAY ENTER

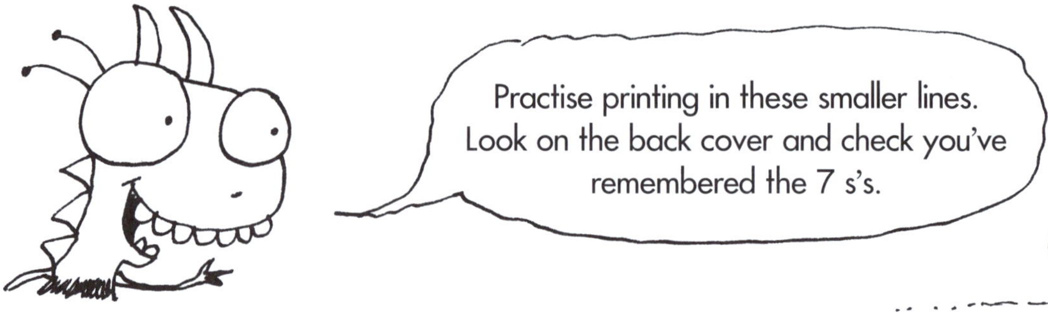

Trace then write.

A wise old owl sat in an oak.

The more he heard the less he spoke.

The less he spoke the more he heard.

Why aren't we all like that wise old bird?

Trace then write the capital letters.

A B C D E F G H I J K L M

N O P Q R S T U V W X Y Z

Handwriting: lower-case and capital printing. **Grammar:** statement, question, sentences. **Punctuation:** capital letters to start sentences, full stops, question mark. **Spelling and vocabulary:** rhyme (heard/bird, oak/spoke). **Literary elements**: Mother Goose rhyme.

Trace then write.

Little Robin Redbreast

sat upon a rail;

Niddle noddle went its head.

Wiggle waggle went its tail.

Trace then write the punctuation marks.

“ ” . . . ? ! – “ ” . . . ? ! – “ ” . . . ? ! –

Trace then write.

“Oooh! Oooh!” exclaimed the owl.

“What did you say?” asked the robin.

Trace then write.

1 2 3 4 5 6 7 8 9 10

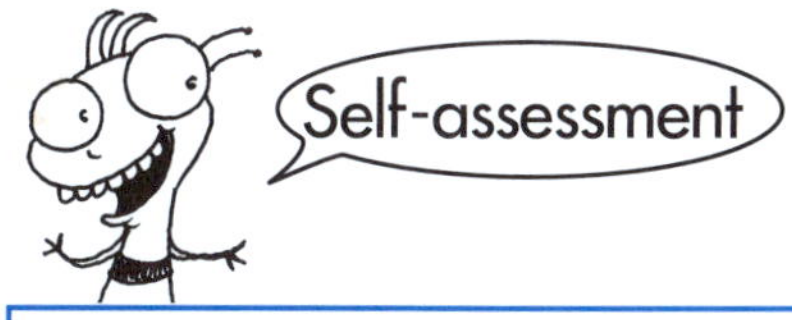

Circle your neatest printed words on this page.

Handwriting: lower-case and capital printing, punctuation, numerals. **Grammar:** statement, exclamation, question, saying verbs (exclaimed, asked). **Punctuation:** sentence punctuation, speech marks, exclamation marks, question marks. **Spelling and vocabulary:** rhyme (rail/tail). **Literary elements**: onomatopoeia, Mother Goose rhyme.

Review: Printing

Choose an adjective and a noun for each label. Remember to print.

Adjectives	awesome, fearsome, loathsome, cumbersome, troublesome, handsome, gruesome
Nouns	teeth, jaws, scales, legs, tail, claws, eyes

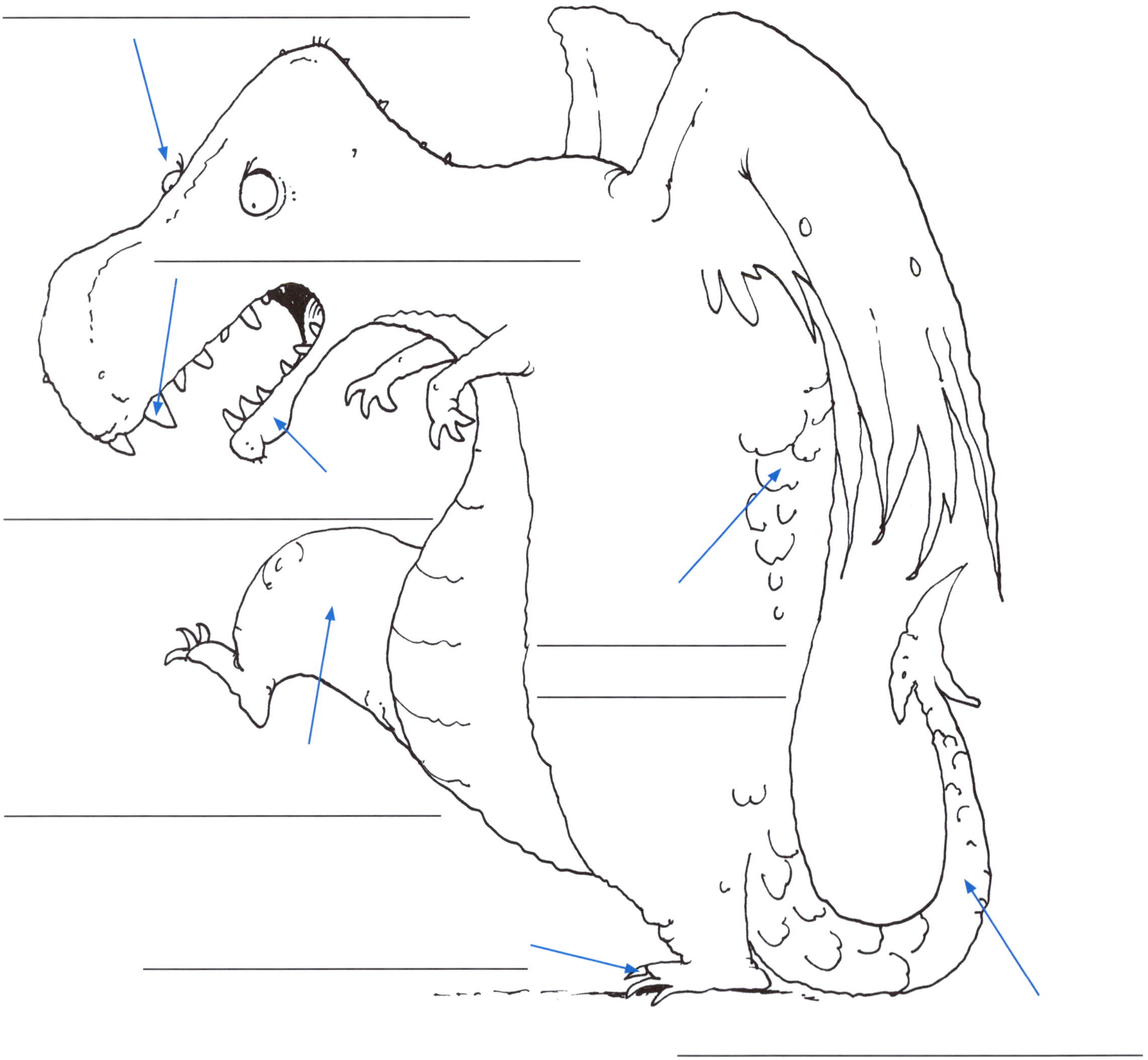

Label any extra parts you like. Give the creature a name.

Handwriting: using printing to label diagrams. **Grammar:** adjectives, nouns, noun groups. **Spelling and vocabulary:** suffix -some. **Literary elements**: mythical creatures (dragons, beasts).

u → u → u → up

Make an exit kick . . . then keep going up . . . until you get to the start of the next letter.

Trace then write. Remember to make smooth diagonal joins.

ar ai aj am an au av aw ay

ap cr ce cu dr du di ei ey

ep eu em en er ew ee hi he

hu hy in im er ki ke kn ky

kr mn mi mu mm my mp ni

ny nu nn ui uy up ur um un

the bee's knees

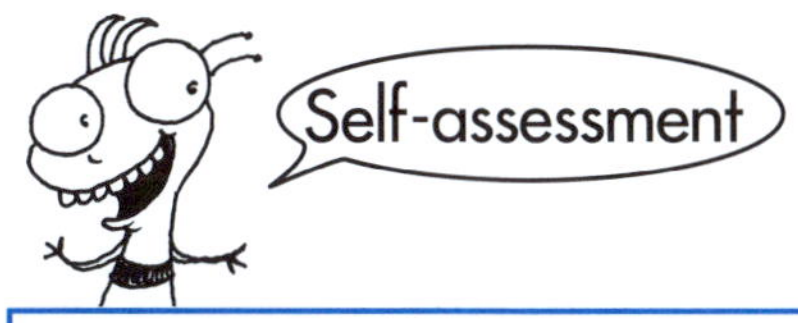

Circle your smoothest join.
Underline a join that needs more practice.

Handwriting: diagonal joins to body and to body and tail letters. **Spelling**: common letter pairs. **Literary elements**: idiom.

Review: Diagonal joins

u → u → u → u   u   ul

Make an exit kick . . . then keep going up . . . to the very top . . . then retrace to make the next letter.

To connect a diagonal join to a tall head and body letter, continue the exit kick all the way up to the top, then retrace to make the next letter.

Trace then write. Be careful when you retrace the join.

ab ah al ak at cl ch ck

ct dt dl dh el et eb ht

hl ik il it ib kl kh ll lk kl

lt mb ml nb nh nt nk nl nb

th tt tl uk ub ut ul at it th

get into hot water

pick of the litter

Self-assessment

My retracing to make joins is improving ☐ good ☐ fantastic ☐.

Handwriting: diagonal joins to head and body letters. **Spelling**: common letter pairs. **Literary elements**: idiom.

Continue the exit kick on the tail of the q all the way up to the top body line.

Trace then write.

qu qu qu qu qu qu qu qu qu qu

The quick queen queued quietly for quoits.

z ↙ little wave

Trace then write.

ze zi zl zu zy zz ze zy

sneeze wheeze freeze breeze squeeze

Write your own words that have a diagonal join from z.

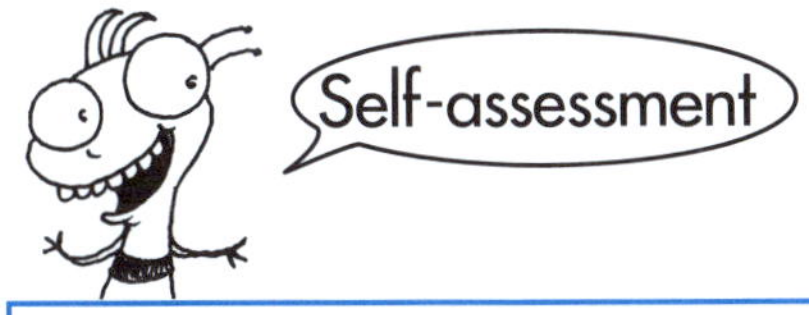

I remembered to make a little wave on z sometimes ☐ often ☐ always ☐.

Handwriting: diagonal joins from q to u, and from z. **Spelling**: common letter pairs, rhyme (sneeze/wheeze/freeze/breeze). **Literary elements**: alliteration.

There's a very funny insect
that you do not often spy.
And it isn't quite a spider
and it isn't quite a fly;
It is something like a beetle,
and a little like a bee,
But nothing like a woolly grub
that climbs upon a tree.
Its name is quite a hard one,
but you'll learn it soon, I hope.
So try: Tri- Tri-anti-wonti
Triantiwontigongolope.

The Triantiwontigongolope

Write the poem. Draw a triantiwontigongolope in the box above.

Handwriting: diagonal joins. **Literary elements**: made-up words, poetry, 'The Triantiwontigongolope', from *A Book for Kids*, by CJ Dennis (1921).

u → u → u → ua

Make an exit kick . . . then keep going up, almost to the top body line . . . then lift your pencil and drop-in the letter.

Trace the letter pairs. Remember to draw a longer exit kick.

ma mo na no uc ic ud id ca da

uq iq ug ig ng nd nc to co do

la lo ta ha ho ka ko ld ad ac

Trace then write.

The ugly duckling turned into a swan.

Only a true Princess can feel a pea beneath 20

mattresses and 20 featherbeds.

Handwriting: drop-in joins after letters with exit kicks. **Punctuation:** sentence punctuation. **Spelling and vocabulary**: plurals adding -s or -es, animal young (ducklings, cygnet). **Literary elements**: references to fairy tales ('The Ugly Duckling', 'The Princess and the Pea', by Hans Christian Andersen).

wi vi ry xy

Trace then write.

oy op on om oz oi ow op on

ry rn ru rm ru ri rr rp ru

vy vu vi vr vu vi vy vu vi

wi wr wu wy wi wr wu wy wn

xi xu xy xy xu xi xy xu xp

Trace then write.

burps like a yowie

wriggles like a viper

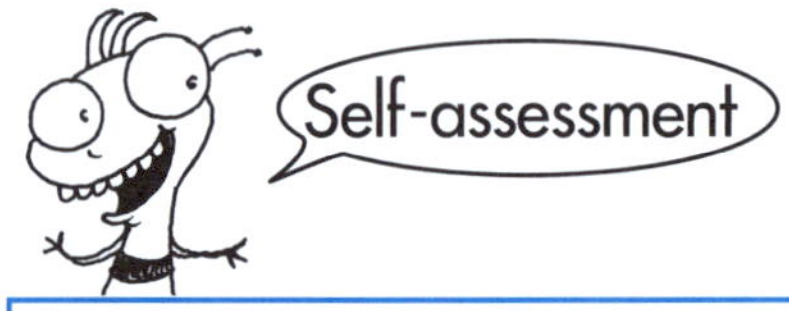

Circle your five best horizontal joins.

Handwriting: horizontal joins. **Spelling:** 'ur' digraph (burp), 'ow' digraph (yowie). **Literary elements**: similes.

Go along the top body line . . . then retrace . . . and write your anticlockwise letter.

Trace then write.

vo va xo xa wa wo va wa wd

oc oa og od oo oa oo oa og od

ro ra rg rd rd rg ra ro ra rg

Trace then write.

rowdy zoom ogre body odd rage crowd

roam moan moat groan rogue toad boat

Trace then write.

The rowdy ogre groaned

as she fell into the moat.

Handwriting: horizontal joins to drop-in letters. **Grammar:** sentences. **Spelling and vocabulary:** 'ow' digraph (rowdy, crowd), 'oa' digraph (groan, moat, moan, toad, boat). **Literary elements**: fantasy character (ogre) and setting (moat), gender representation (she).

Review: Horizontal joins

w → w' → wl → wh

From the exit . . . go up . . . then retrace down.

Trace then write.

ob oh ok ol ol rk rl rt wh ok

howl hoot spooky weird shook whirl disorderly

swirl curl dark disturbing spookish fearless

kooky oddball lurk extraordinary starless broken

Trace then write.

It was very dark and the wind

howled horribly around her.

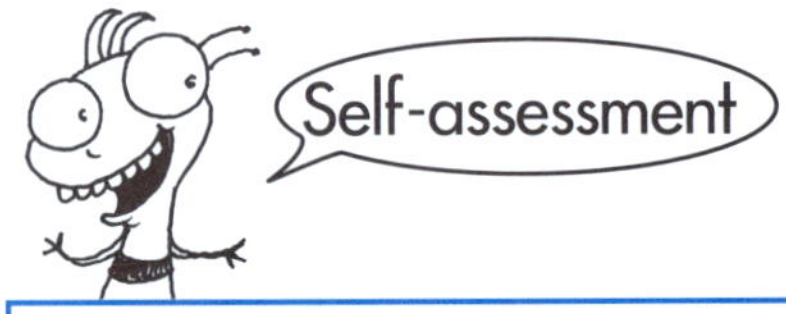

Circle your five best horizontal joins.

Handwriting: horizontal joins to head and body letters. **Grammar:** adjectives (spooky, weird, dark), adverb (horribly). **Spelling and vocabulary:** 'ow', 'oo', 'ir', 'ur', 'ar', 'ur' digraphs. **Literary elements**: alliteration (howled horribly), fantasy settings/scary genre, quote from *The Wonderful Wizard of Oz*, L Frank Baum (1900).

Trace then write.

There was a man in our town,

And he was wondrous wise;

He jumped into a bramble bush,

And scratched out both his eyes;

And when he saw his eyes were out,

With all his might and main

He jumped into another bush,

And scratched them in again.

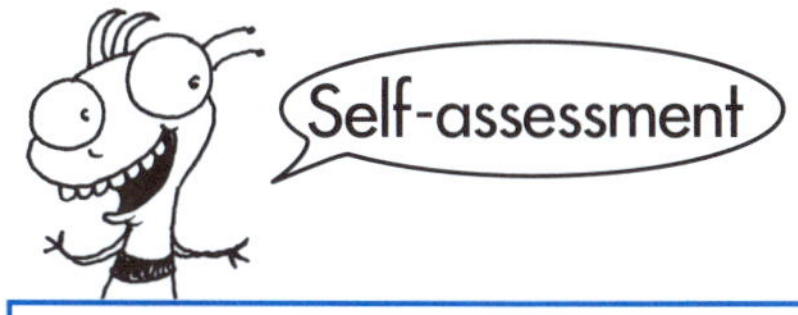

Draw a star next to the line that shows your best writing.
(Think about shape, slope and letter sizes.)

Handwriting: horizontal joins. **Literary elements**: Mother Goose rhyme, idiom 'might and main' meaning 'with all his strength or power' – relevant to time when Mother Goose stories were first published, 1695.

Review: Joins to f

u → u → uf

Go up . . . almost to the top body line . . . then drop-in f.

wf retrace

Trace then write. Remember to lift your pencil.

uf uf   lf lf

ef ef   if if

af af   df df

Trace then write. Remember to retrace the top of the f.

wf wf   xf xf

of of   rf rf

Trace then write.

loafing swift dreadful unsafe awful boxfish

wolf oaf elf waif chief shelf

sniff huff puff bluff surf drift

The awful wolf huffed and puffed.

I remembered when to lift my pencil and when to retrace

sometimes ☐ often ☐ always ☐.

Handwriting: drop-in join to f. **Grammar**: adjectives, nouns, verbs. **Spelling and vocabulary**: common letter pairs, rhyme (huff/puff/bluff, swift/drift). **Literary elements**: reference to folk tale (The Three Pigs).

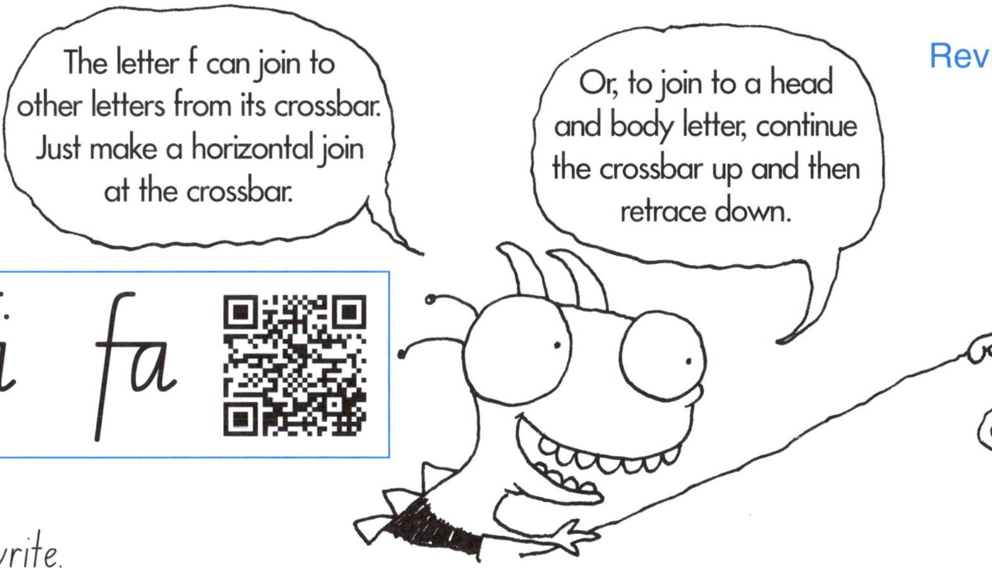

fr fi fa

fl

Trace then write.

fa fa fa

fi fi fi

fo fo fo

fu fu fu

fr fr fr

fy fy fy

fl fl fl

piffle sniffle wiffle waffle

fly flip flop flash flow

terrify magnify specify identify rectify

funny friendly fresh frozen frosty frightened

Handwriting: horizontal joins from f, joining along the crossbar. **Grammar**: verbs, adjectives. **Literary elements**: onomatopoeia.

Trace then write the adjectives. Notice the letters that aren't joined.

black bold beautiful brilliant glowing greedy

gorgeous gentle green giggly gaudy jaunty

jealous juicy jagged jiggly jovial precious

pink pongy paltry pungent pretty putrid

petty happy stripy slimy saggy sensational

skilful shaggy yellow yoghurty yummy yucky

Write some sentences using the adjectives above.

Handwriting: backwards facing letters that don't join yet. **Grammar:** adjectives, sentences. **Spelling and vocabulary**: rhyme (jiggly/giggly, saggy/shaggy), suffix -ful (beautiful, skilful).

Up to now we haven't been joining o, r, v, w or x to e, but there is a way to make a horizontal join. Just make the wavy line dip a little more than it does to other letters.

dip down a little more

oe re ve we xe

Trace then write.

oe re ve we xe oe re ve we xe

oe re ve we xe oe re ve we xe

arrive swerve delve love solve dissolve shove

believe deceive receive leave contrive heave

we're were weren't does doesn't have haven't

"The werewolf doesn't exist."

said the man in the tuxedo.

Handwriting: horizontal joins to e. **Punctuation:** sentence punctuation, speech marks. **Grammar:** verbs. **Spelling and vocabulary**: apostrophes for contraction (we're, weren't, doesn't, haven't). **Literary elements:** reference to *The Bunyip of Berkeley's Creek*, by Jenny Wagner and illustrated by Ron Brooks (1973).

New joins: Horizontal joins to e

Trace then write.

oe re ve we xe oe re ve we xe

Trace then write these adverbs.

carefully incredibly agreeably currently

entirely vertically reliably readily directly

bravely cleverly greedily prettily weekly

dreadfully drearily dreamily realistically

poetically onomatopoeically wearily wetly

Write some sentences using the adverbs above.

Handwriting: horizontal joins to e. **Grammar:** how adverbs ending in -ly, add -ly to change adjectives to adverbs (careful/carefully, incredible/incredibly). **Spelling and vocabulary**: change y to i to add ly (greedy/greedily), double final l before adding ly (dreadful/dreadfully).

Trace then write the words to practise joins to e.

foe goes volcanoes tomatoes heroes

woeful whoever wrongdoer does joey

answer cobwebs welcome weary superpower

allowed sweaty tower webbed paperweight

above clever government curve forever

develop forgive invertebrate vegetable never

address admire firefighter

adventure breeze derelict

hoaxes exercise taxes

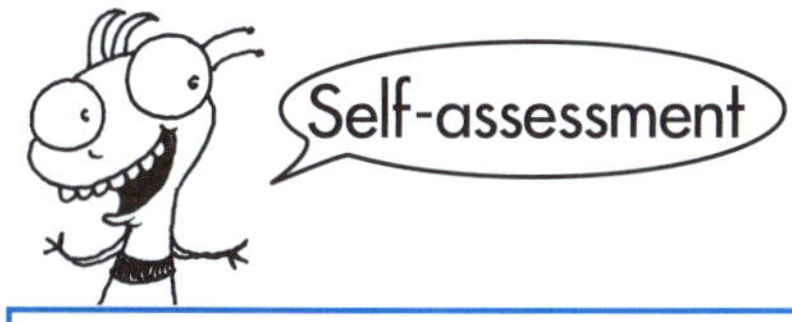

Underline any horizontal joins to e that you could improve.

Handwriting: horizontal joins to e. **Spelling and vocabulary:** compound words (firefighter, paperweight), add -es to words that end in o to make plural.

ox

From o, use a horizontal exit with a wavy line.

ax ux ix ex

From a, u, i and e, use a diagonal join.

Trace then write.

ox ox ox ox ox ox ox ox ox ox ox ox ox

ax ax ax ax ax ax ax ax ax ax ax ax

ux ux ux ux ux ux ux ux ux ux ux ux

ix ix ix ix ix ix ix ix ix ix ix ix ix ix

ex ex ex ex ex ex ex ex ex ex ex ex ex

mix fix fox fax flux flex flax text exit

flummox reflux moxie pixie pixels exhaust

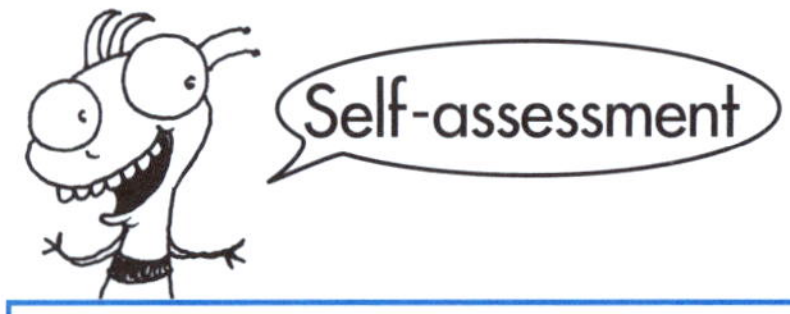

Put a cross next to any joins to x that you could improve.

Handwriting: horizontal and diagonal joins to x. **Spelling and vocabulary**: x says 'ks' in each word on this page.

Trace then write.

ox

ax

ux

ix

ex

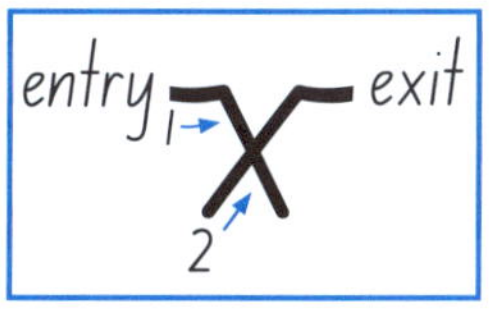

Trace. Then choose two of the adjectives and write sentences of your own.

exciting excellent exceptional exhilarating

obnoxious exhausted deluxe maximum express

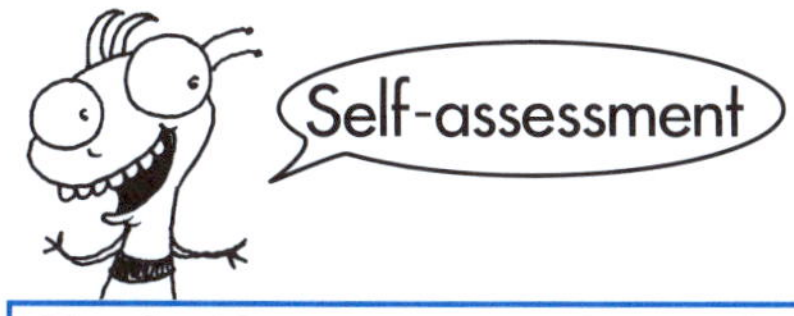

Circle your five best joins on the page.

Handwriting: joins to and from x. **Grammar:** adjectives.

To write faster, you can join s from letters that finish at the top body line. Make a horizontal join and then retrace the top of the s.

o → o → os (retrace) → os

Extend the exit hook over the top of the s . . . then retrace back around.

Trace then write.

os os os os os os os os os os os os os os

fs fs fs fs fs fs fs fs fs fs fs fs fs fs fs

rs rs rs rs rs rs rs rs rs rs rs rs rs rs

Trace then write these adverbs.

possibly positively loosely mostly crossly

Trace then write the sentences.

"I'm positive it could possibly rain," said Sam.

The oafs wore scarfs and briefs.

Self-assessment

Tick any joins to s that are excellent.

Underline any joins that you could improve.

Handwriting: horizontal joins to s. **Punctuation:** sentence punctuation, speech marks, proper noun (Sam). **Grammar:** how adverbs ending in -ly, modality (possibly). **Spelling and vocabulary**: suffix -ly (possibly, positively, loosely, mostly, crossly).

Trace then write.

pianos banjos solos cellos sopranos discos

mangos avocados autos limos kangaroos

roofs dwarfs beliefs cliffs castoffs reefs

advisors cleaners managers smugglers

moss post whose nose utmost rose

sniffs snuffs whiffs hoofs bluffs huffs puffs

course coarse thirst first juniors radars

Handwriting: horizontal joins to s. **Spelling and vocabulary**: mangos, mangoes, avocados and avocadoes are all correct, homophones (course/coarse), musical terms ending in o just add ‘s’ (pianos), jobs often end in ‘er’, ‘or’ or ‘ist’ (cleaners, advisors, dentists).

New joins: Diagonal joins to s

Here's a new fast way to make a diagonal join to s. The shape of the s is a little different.

Trace then write.

a → a → as

top of s is much shorter

Make a diagonal exit kick . . . keep going to make a short top on the s . . . then quickly retrace around.

as as as as as as as as as as as as peas

is is is is is is is is is is is is is is fish

ns ns ns ns ns ns ns ns ns ns ns beans

ls ls ls ls ls ls ls ls ls ls ls ls ls ls trolls

ts ts ts ts ts ts ts ts ts ts ts ts ts hats

es es es es es es es es es es es es shoes

Trolls wearing hats and shoes ate

fish with peas and beans.

Self-assessment

Tick any diagonal joins to s that are excellent.

Underline any joins that you could improve.

Handwriting: diagonal joins to s, new s shape.

Practise diagonal joins with these plurals. Trace then write.

snakes lizards walruses kisses prizes

batteries apologies activities dragonflies

countries heroes volcanoes potatoes

loaves thieves knives

hooves elves calves

Trace then write.

"The time has come," the Walrus said,

"To talk of many things:

Of shoes – and ships – and sealing-wax –

Of cabbages – and kings."

Handwriting: diagonal joins to s. **Punctuation:** sentence punctuation, speech marks. **Spelling and vocabulary**: plurals adding -s, -es, -ies. **Literary elements:** quote from *Through the Looking Glass*, by Lewis Carroll (1872).

Consolidation: Double letters without joins

Trace then write the compound words.

cubbyhouse steppingstone eggshell cubbyhole

piggyback grasshopper passionfruit passport

Find and write words of your own that use these double letters.

gg pp

ss bb

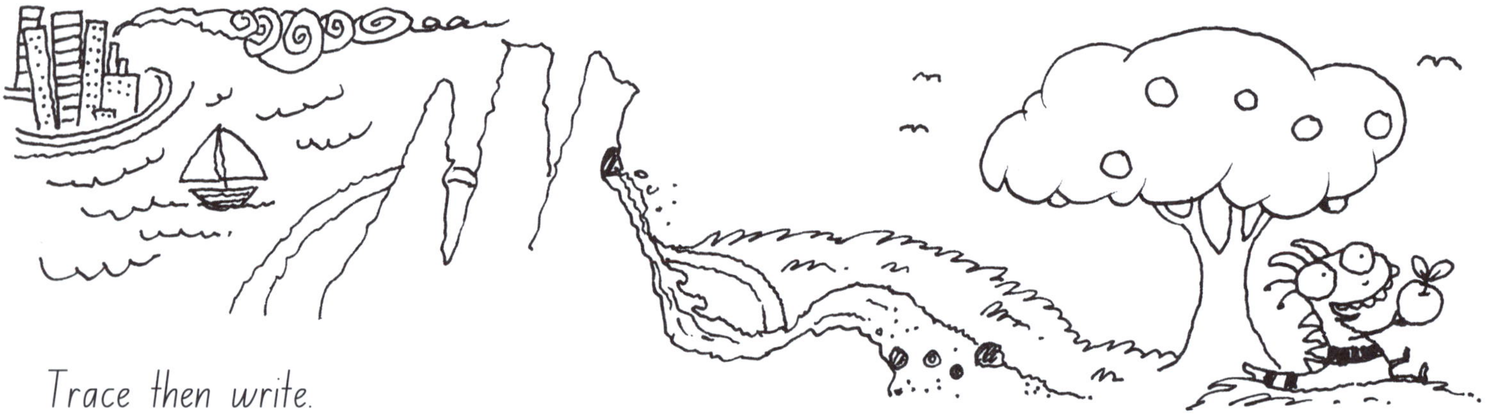

Trace then write.

Out of the smoggy city, across the choppy sea, over the

rugged mountains, down the slippery slope, into the

pebbly stream, through the grassy field, for an apple.

My writing on this page is improving good fantastic .

Handwriting: double letters that don't join together yet. **Punctuation:** commas to separate phrases. **Grammar:** prepositions, prepositional phrases, adjectives, common nouns. **Spelling and vocabulary**: compound words (eggshell, passport).

Trace then write.

cc

dd

oo

ll

mm

nn

ee

rr

tt

ff

Trace then write.

accepting adding stooping pulling humming

running sleeping slurring hitting puffing

Write some words of your own with double letters that join together.

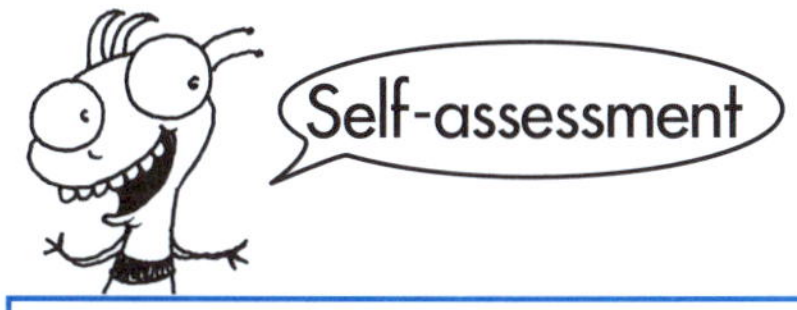

Underline any joins that you could improve.

Handwriting: double letters that join together. **Grammar:** verbs, tense. **Spelling and vocabulary**: double final consonant to add -ing (hit/hitting, run/running).

Consolidation: double letters that join together

Trace then write these compound words.

overall wallpaper overrun waterproof treetop

strawberry rattlesnake toadstool seaweed

jellyfish sheepdog kneecap seagull foolproof

hummingbird toothbrush moonbeam goodnight

Trace then write the similes.

A cat's purr is beautiful,

like a strange lullaby.

Prrrrrr . . . Prrrrrr . . .

A cat's purr feels

like a car's motor running.

Handwriting: double letters that join together. **Grammar**: possessive apostrophes (cat's, car's). **Punctuation:** ellipsis (. . .). **Spelling and vocabulary:** compound words. **Literary elements:** similes, quote from *The Five Lives of our Cat Zook*, by Joanne Rocklin (2012).

Trace then write these words that are often misspelt. How fast can you write them without making any spelling mistakes and still be neat?

about
always
because
cannot
coming
doesn't
enough
excited
guess
heard
laugh
often
quiet
until

almost
answer
before
clothes
doctor
eighth
except
friend
having
know
might
people
quite
tonight

Don't lose those loose wheels.

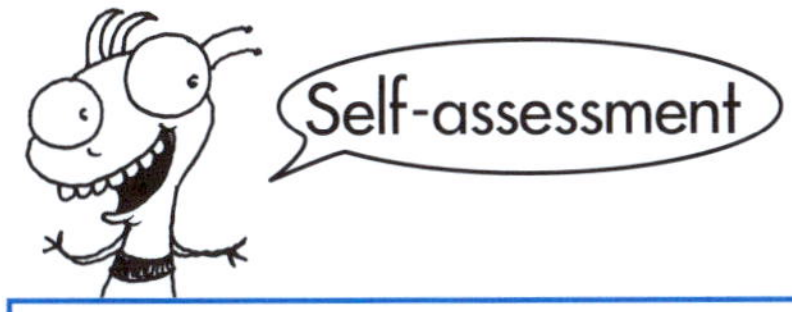

Circle five words that show your writing is fluent and legible.

Handwriting: all joins, legibility. **Spelling and vocabulary**: frequently misspelt words.

A **palindrome** is a word, phrase or sentence that reads the same forwards or backwards.

Trace then write the palindrome words.

bib	dad	deed
did	dud	eve
eye	gag	gig
kayak	level	madam
mum	nan	noon
peep	pip	pop
pup	radar	redder

Trace then write the palindrome phrases and sentences. Then write some palindromes of your own.

race car

swap paws

snack cans

stunt nuts

Too bad I hid a boot.

Race fast, safe car.

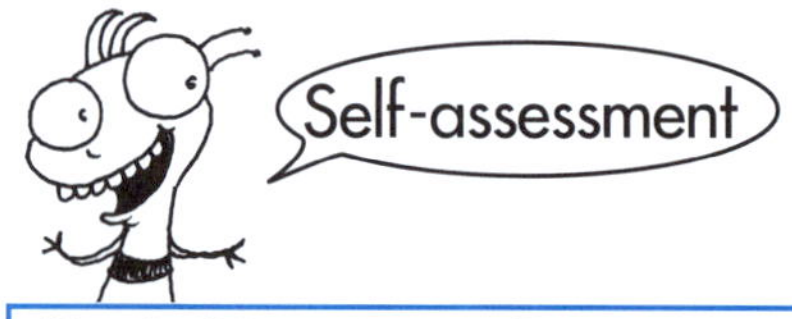

Tick your best joins.
Put a cross next to any joins that need more practice.

Handwriting: all joins. **Grammar**: sentences. **Literary elements**: palindromes.

Trace then write each adjective. Then write your own adjectives to describe how something **looks**.

grotesque multicoloured crooked sparkling dirty

Trace then write each adjective. Then write your own adjectives to describe how something **sounds**.

blaring hushed squeaking raspy muffled loud

Trace then write each adjective. Then write your own adjectives to describe how something **tastes**.

bitter delicious sour yummy tangy unripe

Trace then write each adjective. Then write your own adjectives to describe how something **smells**.

perfumed putrid noxious musty burnt smoky

Trace then write each adjective. Then write your own adjectives to describe how something **feels**.

fluffy fuzzy prickly sticky damp slippery

Handwriting: all joins. **Grammar**: adjectives. **Literary elements**: descriptions that make use of the senses.

1 Pick a genre.

scary ☐ adventure ☐ historical ☐
mystery ☐ fantasy ☐ funny ☐

2 Draw a map of a possible setting for a story in your chosen genre.

3 Add labels. Include labels to describe what you might see, hear, smell, feel and taste if you were standing in this setting.

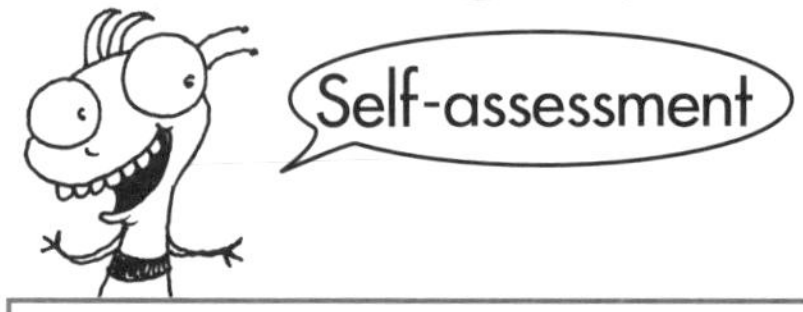

My printing on this page is improving ☐ good ☐ fantastic ☐ .

Handwriting: using printing to label maps and diagrams. **Literary elements**: genre, setting, descriptions.

An **anagram** is a word or phrase made by changing the order of the letters in another word or phrase.

Trace then write the anagrams.

astronomers = no more stars

the eyes = they see

mummy = my mum

the countryside = no city dust here

conversation = voices rant on

twelve plus one = eleven plus two

vacation time = I am not active

My writing slopes in the same direction
sometimes ☐ often ☐ always ☐.

Handwriting: all joins, consistent slope. **Grammar**: phrases. **Literary elements**: anagrams.

Consolidation: Speed and fluency, legibility

Trace then write.

said

he

she

they

his

her

their

your

can

could

will

from

where

when

which

who

what

These words are from a list of 100 most used words that make up about half of all reading and writing.

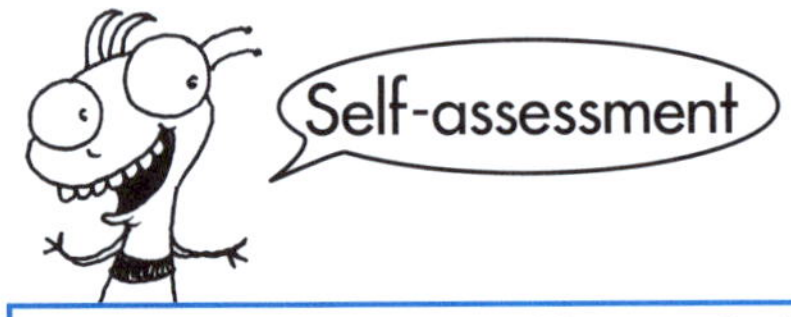

On each line: Draw a star above the word you wrote the fastest. Tick the word you wrote the neatest.

Handwriting: speed and fluency, legibility. **Spelling and vocabulary**: common words.

Trace then write the different ways to say 'said'.

announced argued asked babbled

barked bawled bellowed bleated

blurted called chattered cheered

croaked drawled growled grumbled

hissed muttered piped quavered

ranted roared shouted sighed

snapped sobbed stammered whimpered

Write your own words to use instead of 'said'.

Handwriting: all joins. **Grammar**: saying verbs. **Spelling and vocabulary**: synonyms. **Literary elements**: words for said.

Interjections are words that show emotion or feelings. They can stand alone.

Trace then write the interjections for each emotion. Write one in each speech bubble.

angry: grrr agh humph

happy: bravo eureka yippee

sad: aw alas drat

worried: uh oh oops oh no

questioning: hey eh huh

scared: eek ahhhh yikes

relieved: phew golly whoa

Trace then write a sentence to follow each interjection.

Eek!

Yippee!

Handwriting: all joins. **Grammar**: interjections.

Trace the nouns for items in the kitchen. Then, for each letter of the alphabet, write your own noun for something in your home.

almonds	bok choy	curry	dumplings
a	b	c	d
eggflip	forks	garbage	herbs
e	f	g	h
ice	juice	knives	lemons
i	j	k	l
mushrooms	nuts	oranges	plates
m	n	o	p
quinces	radishes	sausages	tangerines
q	r	s	t
utensils	vegetables	watermelon	
u	v	w	
toxic mould	yoghurt	zucchinis	
x	y	z	

Choose four kitchen items. Write them here with a describing adjective for each one, for example sour lemons.

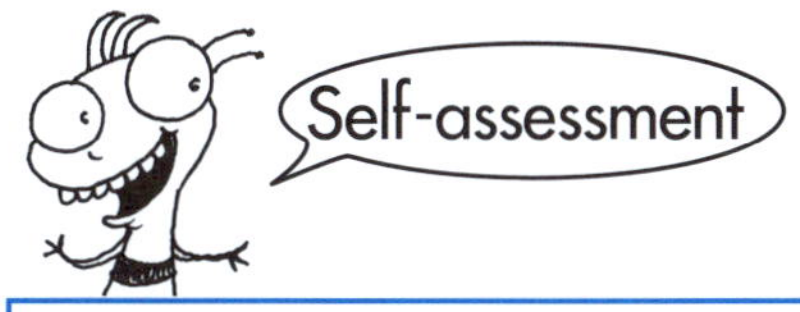

Circle five words that show your writing is fluent and legible.

Handwriting: all joins. **Grammar:** nouns, adjectives. **Spelling and vocabulary**: different types of plurals -es (radishes), -s (lemons), no change from singular to plural (bok choy, garbage, ice, yoghurt, mould).

Consolidation: all joins

Remember to keep your letter shape, size, slope and spacing consistent.

Trace then write the thinking verbs.

hope hoped wished wondered believed

Trace then write.

Thomas sat in the doctor's waiting room, trying not

to panic about his arm. It wasn't looking good.

A red stain was seeping through the bandage.

Oops, thought Thomas. I think I used too much jam.

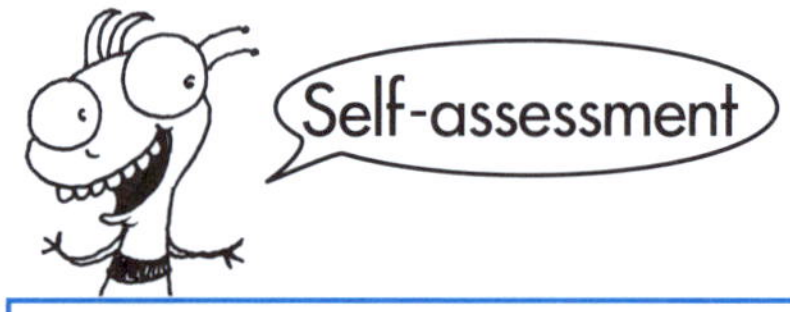

Cross out the words that don't apply.

I need to work on my letter shapes, slope, spacing, size, tails.

Handwriting: all joins. **Grammar**: thinking verbs (thought, think), apostrophe for possession (doctor's), proper noun (Thomas). **Spelling and vocabulary**: apostrophes for contraction (wasn't), homophone (too/to/two). **Literary elements:** third person narrative, point of view, quote from *Doubting Thomas*, by Morris Gleitzman (2006).

Trace then write.

sch scr spl spr shr sph squ str thr

sch school scr scream spl splat

spr sprint shr shriek sph sphere

squ square str straight thr through

Find and write a word of your own for each letter cluster.

sch scr spl

spr shr sph

squ str thr

Trace then write.

Characters in scary movies

shriek and scream.

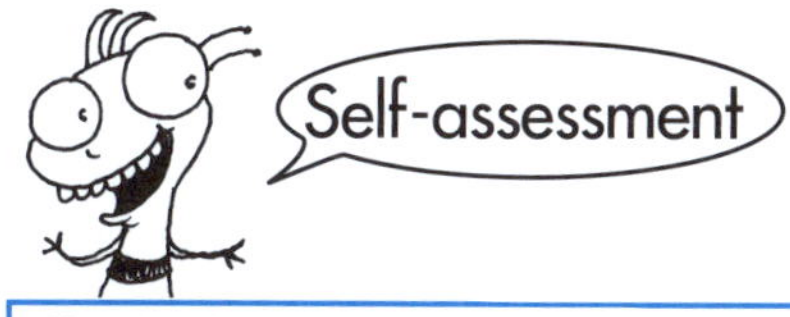

Put a cross next to any joins that you could improve.

Handwriting: all joins. **Spelling and vocabulary:** three letter consonant blends 'spl', 'spr'.

Consolidation: all joins

Trace then write.

au aw or ai ay ea ee ei er oa

ou eu ew ey ie oi oo ou ow oy

au automatic aw awful or short sport fort

ai straight ay day slay ea meat cheat bleat

ee cheek ei eight er germ oa boat oath

ow power shower eu eureka ew drew slew

ey prey grey ie pie die oi toil boil avoid

oo scoot ou shout oy boy

Write words that rhyme.

port	pleat	flew
stay	tower	spoil
lie	peek	float

Handwriting: all joins. **Spelling and vocabulary:** 'au', 'ai', 'oi', 'ea', 'ee', 'oa', 'ei', 'ie', 'eu', 'ou', 'oo', 'aw', 'or', 'er', 'ew', 'ow', 'ey', 'ay', 'oy' digraphs for vowel sounds.

Trace then write.

first second third fourth fifth sixth

seventh eighth ninth tenth hundredth

tle castle rustle dge dodge ght night flight

nk stink tion nation motion lk stalk talk

Write words of your own which use the letter patterns.

tle dge ght

nk tion lk

Choose a homophone from the box for each word below.

whale would know eight flower through hair
creak steel boy choose fur stalk piece sale

peace steal no

ate wood hare

wail flour creek

threw buoy chews

fir stork sail

Handwriting: all joins. **Spelling and vocabulary**: homophones, letter patterns -tle, -tion, -ght, -dge, -nk, -lk.

Consolidation: all joins

Trace. Then choose a prefix from the box to write an antonym beside each word.

un im ir il dis

known	possible	tidy
practical	natural	obedient
intentional	stable	like
qualify	believable	agree
approve	able	regular
rational	mature	obey

Trace. Then add a suffix from the box to each word.
Some words might be able to use more than one suffix.

ful less able

hope	care	paper
help	effort	waste
wish	thought	dread
approach	fear	answer
spot	mind	count
fix	kiss	taste

Trace. Then write these words with silent letters.

thumb	scene	gnaw
knock	autumn	whistle
guitar	guess	wrestle

Handwriting: all joins **Spelling and vocabulary**: antonyms, negative prefixes un-, im-, ir-, il-, dis-, suffixes -ful, -less, -able, silent letters (thumb, scene, gnaw, knock, autumn, whistle, guitar, guess, wrestle).

A **pangram** is a sentence that uses every letter of the alphabet. You can use letters more than once.

Trace then write these pangrams.

The wolf just kept dozing very
quietly in a crumpled box.

The mad taxi driver wove quickly past the frisky
zebra crossing the road.

A big killer ox squashed the very cute jumping
frogs as they did a waltz.

Write a pangram of your own.

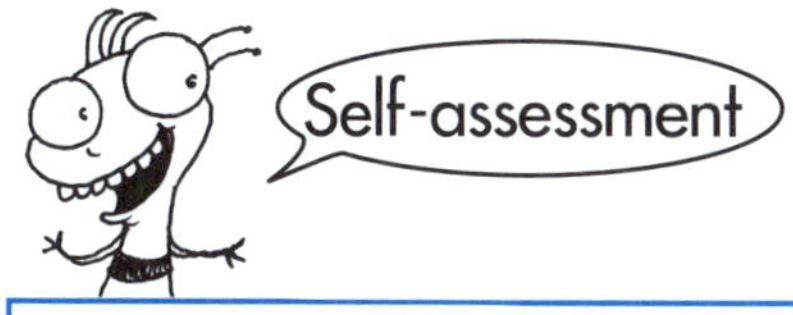

Cross out the words that don't apply.
I need to work on my letter shapes, slope, spacing, size, tails.

Handwriting: all joins. **Literary elements:** pangrams.

Consolidation: all joins

Trace then write these sentences about classic stories.

Make sure your writing arm and hand can move freely. Keep your pencil or pen hold relaxed and flexible.

The children entered Narnia

through a wardrobe in the spare room.

A cyclone whirled Dorothy

and Toto to the Land of Oz.

Gulliver was washed ashore in Lilliput.

Peter Pan and Tinkerbell flew to Neverland.

Alice fell into a rabbit-hole and

discovered Wonderland.

Write a sentence of your own that tells how a story character entered a fantasy world.

Handwriting: all joins. **Grammar:** proper nouns (Narnia, Dorothy, Toto, Land of Oz, Gulliver, Lilliput, Peter Pan, Tinkerbell, Neverland, Alice, Wonderland), prepositional phrases (through a wardrobe, in the spare room), verbs (whirled, was washed). **Literary elements**: fantasy genre, characters and settings, entering fantasy worlds, references to *The Lion, the Witch and the Wardrobe*, C S Lewis (1950), *The Wonderful Wizard of Oz*, L Frank Baum (1900), *Gulliver's Travels*, Jonathan Swift (1726), *Peter Pan*, JM Barrie (1911), *Alice's Adventures in Wonderland*, Lewis Carroll (1865). (Note, these books have all been made into films.)

Trace then write the similes.

as scarce as hen's teeth

as bold as brass

as clear as mud

as nutty as a fruit cake

Trace then write the lines from a playscript.
Scene: Shaggy man and Button-bright face the Scoodlers.

Shaggy man: What do you want?

Scoodlers (yelling, pointing): You!

Shaggy man: What do you want us for?

Scoodlers (shouting): Soup!

Button-bright (crying): Don't want to be soup.

Handwriting: all joins. **Grammar:** questions, exclamation, statement, proper nouns (Shaggy man, Scoodlers, Button-bright). **Punctuation:** colons, brackets, exclamation marks, question marks. **Literary elements**: similes, tongue-in-cheek humour, irony, colloquialism, stage directions, characters, playscript adapted from Chapter 9, 'Facing the Scoodlers', from *The Road to Oz*, L Frank Baum (1909).

Consolidation: all joins

Trace then write these words for plants and animals.

kangaroo bogong wallaroo wallaby dingo

galah currawong bunyip boobook bilby

pademelon quokka quoll waratah wombat

yabby kookaburra

wobbegong numbat

brolga taipan

budgerigar myall mallee

mulga potoroo witchetty koala drongo quandong

barramundi coolabah kurrajong gang-gang

Handwriting: all joins. **Spelling and vocabulary**: etymology, words in English from Aboriginal languages.

Print the labels on the map.

1 Mundaring	2 Karratha	3 Pilbara	4 Jabiru	5 Kalgoorlie
6 Coolgardie	7 Yulara	8 Nhulunbuy	9 Aurukun	10 Tanunda
11 Cocklebiddy	12 Biloela	13 Noosa	14 Maroochydore	15 Currumbin
16 Arakoon	17 Wilcannia	18 Dubbo	9 Uralla	20 Turramurra
21 Parramatta	22 Ballarat	23 Thirroul	24 Geelong	25 Wonthaggi
26 Canberra				

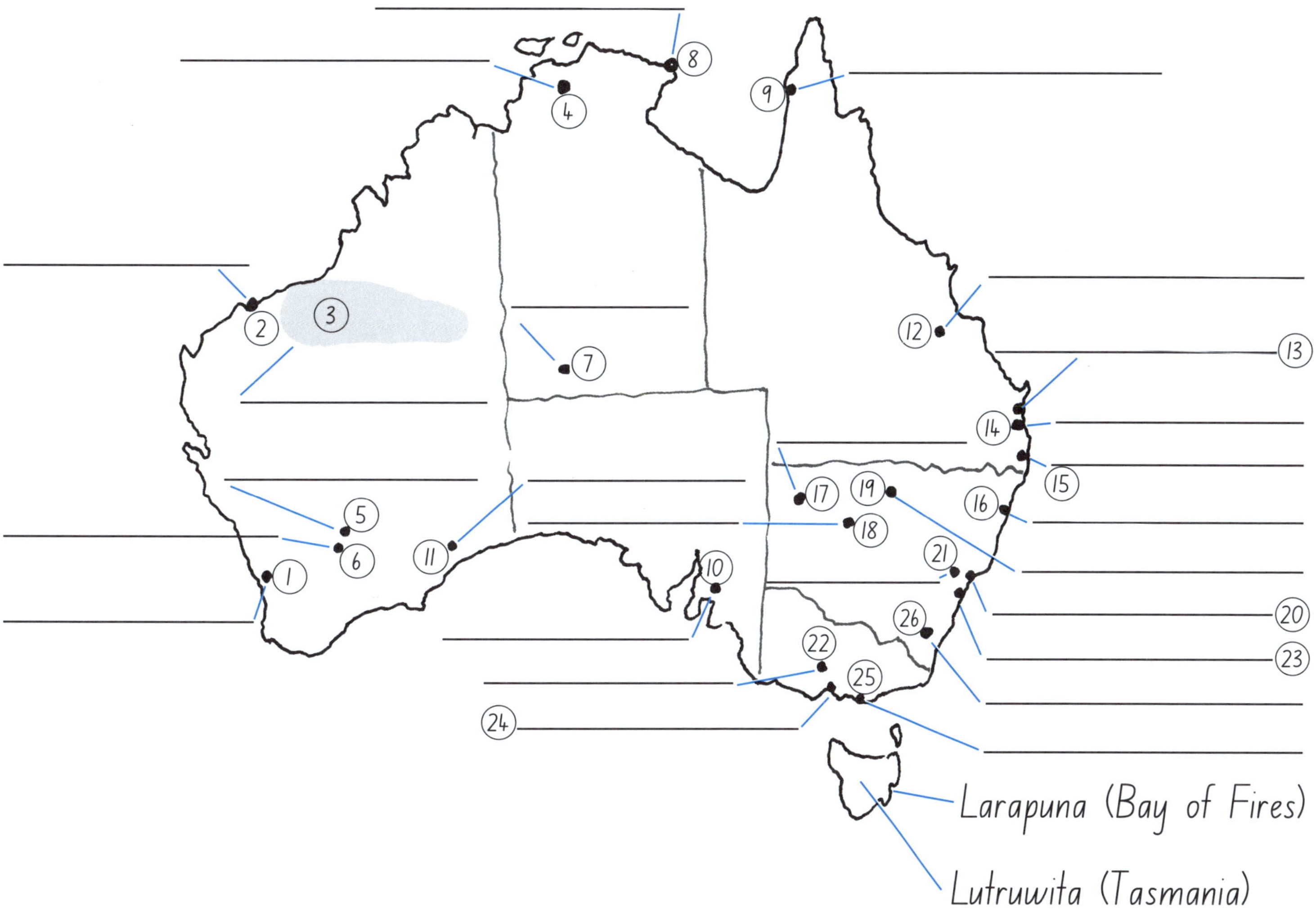

Complete the crime scene report to investigate what happened to Humpty Dumpty. Did Humpty fall or was it foul play?

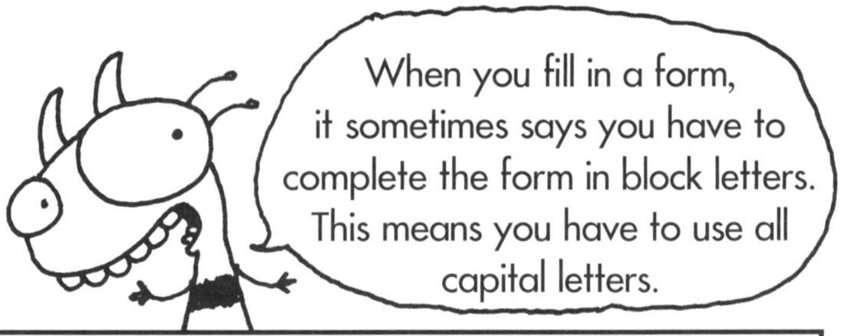

CRIME SCENE REPORT

TO BE COMPLETED IN BLOCK LETTERS

TYPE OF CRIME	
WHERE CRIME TOOK PLACE	
TIME CRIME TOOK PLACE	
VICTIM DETAILS	
DESCRIPTION OF CRIME SCENE	
EVIDENCE COLLECTED	
WITNESS NAME	
WITNESS STATEMENT	

Handwriting: capitals. **Literary elements:** common expression (foul play).

Here are some new guidelines to try.

Remember to keep your tall letters, and letters with tails, a consistent size!

Trace then write the sentences. Finish each sentence with a character name from the box.

Rapunzel	Goldilocks	The Wolf	Jack	Baby Bear

"Oh! Someone ate my porridge," cried ______________.

"I'll blow your house down," shouted ______________.

"Oops! I broke the chair," said ______________.

"I'll hang down my hair," said ______________.

"Yikes! The Giant is coming!" yelled ______________.

Write a sentence of your own for each character in the box.

Cinderella	The Little Mermaid	Red Riding Hood	Grandma	Aladdin

Handwriting: all joins, maintaining letter size without head and tail guidelines. **Grammar:** interjections, exclamations, dialogue, saying verbs (cried, shouted, yelled, said), proper nouns (Goldilocks, Cinderella, Alladin). **Punctuation:** speech marks, exclamation marks. **Literary elements**: fairy tales, story characters.

New guidelines

Trace then write. Finish the speech bubbles.

The solemn gnome hurt his thumb whilst making

fudge on Wednesday. He had to guard the dessert from

the naughty knight at the castle, so he climbed a cliff

and hid it under some thistles. He ate the fudge after

an hour, leaving no crumbs.

Handwriting: all joins, maintaining letter size without head or tail guidelines. **Spelling and vocabulary:** words with silent letters (solemn, gnome, thumb, Wednesday, guard, naughty, knight, castle, climbed, thistles, hour, crumbs), fudge uses dge to make a j sound, desert/dessert often confused. **Literary elements**: fantasy characters (gnome, knight, dragon).

Check your letter size, slope and spacing as you write.

New guidelines

Trace then write.

The accused biter hopped into a tiny tinny. He took

his rabbit and his kitten, too. All of a sudden his

rudder shuddered having jammed into an alligator.

It was difficult to steer and he slammed into some

jagged rocks. His canny granny pulled his boat to

shore. He commented, later, that he'd seen the error

of his ways.

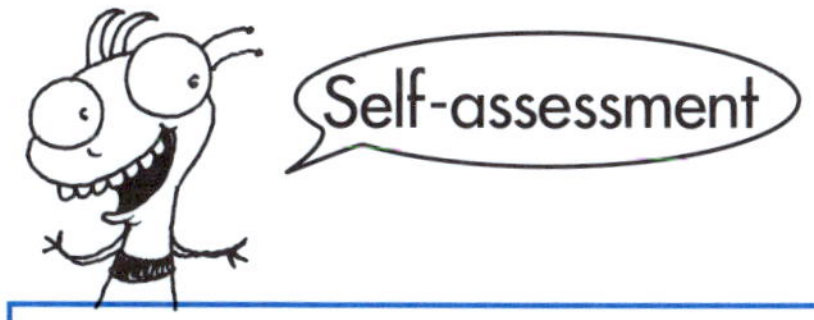

Rate your writing out of 10:

fluency ____ speed ____ legibility ____

Handwriting: joined double letters ee, cc, dd, ff, ll, mm, nn, oo, rr, ff, unjoined double letters bb, gg, ss, pp, maintaining letter size without head and tail guidelines. **Spelling and vocabulary:** common mistakes (tiny/tinny, hopped/hoped), rhyme (rudder/shudder, slammed/jammed).

Trace then write this stanza from a Henry Lawson poem.

It leapt across the flaming streams

And raced the pastures through;

It climbed the trees, and lit the boughs,

And fierce and fiercer grew.

The bees fell stifled in the smoke

Or perished in their hives,

And with the stock the kangaroos

Went flying for their lives.

Handwriting: all joins, maintaining letter size without head and tail guidelines. **Spelling and vocabulary:** 'ough' (through, bough). **Literary elements:** poetry, quote from 'The Fire at Ross's Farm', published in *The Days When The World Was Wide*, by Henry Lawson (1900).

Write the limericks in your best joined writing. Draw an illustration for each limerick.

There was an old man in a barge,
Whose nose was exceedingly large;
But in fishing by night, it supported a light,
Which helped that old man in a barge.

There was a young lady of Greenwich,
Whose garments were border'd with Spinach;
But a large spotty Calf bit her shawl quite in half,
Which alarmed that young lady of Greenwich.

Handwriting: all joins, maintaining letter size without head and tail guidelines. **Grammar:** possessive pronoun (whose). **Punctuation:** capital to start each line of a poem, semicolons. **Literary elements:** limericks, 'There Was an Old Man in a Barge', 'There was a Young Lady of Greenwich', from *More Nonsense, Pictures, Rhymes, Botany &c*, by Edward Lear (1872).

bi pi sl

retrace

Retrace the bottom of the letter. Then go up to make a diagonal join to the next letter.

Write.

ba be bo bu bi br by pa pe pi

pn po pr pu py sa sc se si sa

sm sn so sp sq su sw sy so su

bl ph pl sh sk sl st bl pl sh

Write the anagram pairs.

bear bare blame amble

please elapse pastel staple

Write your own anagram.

bowl post seal

Handwriting: fluency joins from b, p and s. **Spelling and vocabulary**: common letter pairs. **Literary elements**: anagrams.

bb pp ss

Write.

bb pp ss

babble dabble sobbed dripped

slipped suppose gossip guess

Peter Piper picked a peck of pickled peppers;

A peck of pickled peppers Peter Piper picked;

If Peter Piper picked a peck of pickled peppers,

Where's the peck of pickled peppers

Peter Piper picked?

Self-assessment

My retracing to make joins is improving ☐ good ☐ fantastic ☐ .

Handwriting: joining double b, p and s. **Grammar**: verbs (babble, dabble), past tense (sobbed, dripped, picked, pickled). **Spelling**: double letters. **Literary elements**: tongue twisters.

Cross the loop at the top body line.

al ol

Using a speed loop to a tall head and body letter means you don't have to retrace the tall letter carefully.

Write the letter pairs. Try using speed loops.

ab ah al eh el ib ik il ob

ol ub uh ul dl rl tl wl

Write the anagram pairs.

lump plum bruise rubies

horse shore weak wake

Write the tongue twister.

She sells sea shells by the sea shore.

The shells she sells are seashells, I'm sure.

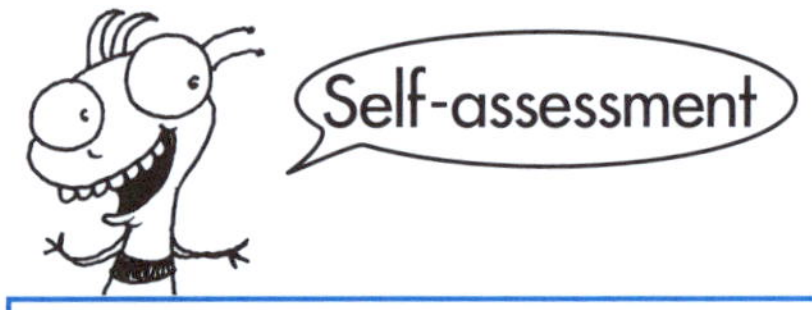

My speed loops cross at the top body line

sometimes ☐ often ☐ always ☐.

Handwriting: speed loops to head and body letters b, h, k and l. **Literary elements**: anagrams, tongue twisters.

gi ji yi

Cross the loop at the baseline.

Write the letters.

g g g ga ge gh gi gl go gr gu

j j j ja je ji jo ju ja je ji jo ju

y y y ya ye yi yo yu yl yr

Write the anagram pairs.

garden danger grin ring gulp plug

night thing jest jets yap pay

Write the tongue twisters.

Granny's grey goose goes last.

A gentle judge judges justly.

My speed loops cross at the baseline sometimes ☐ often ☐ always ☐.

Handwriting: speed loops from tail letters g, j and y. **Literary elements**: anagrams, alliteration, tongue twisters.

from often

Add the crossbar when you finish the word.

Write the letters.

f f f f f fa fe fi fo fu

af ef if of uf ift ify eft uff

Write an anagram for each word.

flee fringe

fits file

foul softer

cafe fare

framed flea

Write.

The furry fly flitted through fifty flowers.

Five frantic frogs fled from fifty fierce fishes.

Handwriting: speed loops to and from f. **Literary elements**: anagrams, alliteration, tongue twisters.

Write.

In the High and Far-Off Times the Elephant,

O Best Beloved, had no trunk. He had only a blackish,

bulgy nose, as big as a boot, that he could wriggle

about from side to side; but he couldn't pick up

things with it.

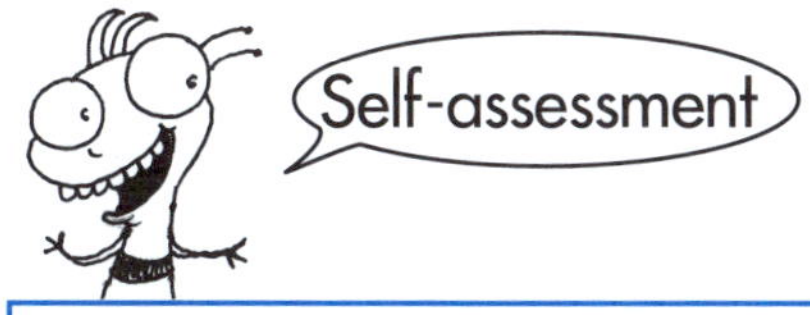

Rate your writing out of 10: fluency _____ speed _____ legibility _____ .

Handwriting: practising all speed loops. **Grammar**: adjectives (blackish, bulgy). **Literary elements**: quote from 'The Elephant's Child' from *Just So Stories*, by Rudyard Kipling (1902), simile (as big as a boot).

Experiment with different ways to sign your name.

Choose your favourite signature. Practise writing it on the lines.
Try to write each signature exactly the same.

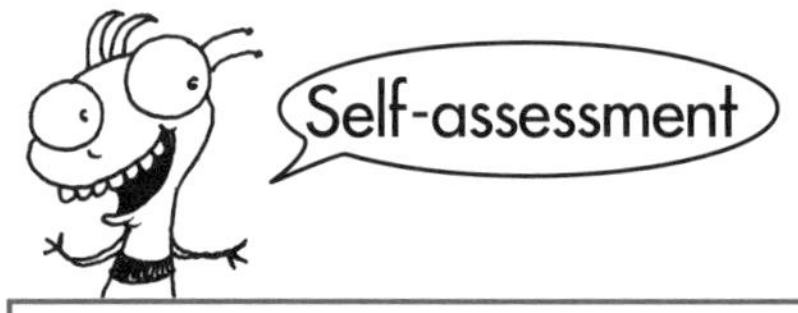

Circle your favourite signature.

Handwriting: developing own personal style.

Collect autographs from your classmates and teachers.

An autograph is someone's signature.

You can stamp and rage,
I'm still first on this page.

You'd better write fast,
or you'll be the last!

Have a classmate time you as you rewrite the sentence from the box. Use all the joins you have learned. Make sure you write as fluently and legibly as you can.

Grumpy dancers caught a quick taxi to Wonthaggi to juggle volleyballs for the crazy human circus.

Assessment 1

Date ____________ Time ______ minutes ______ seconds

Assessment 2

Date ____________ Time ______ minutes ______ seconds

Assessment 3

Date ____________________ Time _______ minutes _______ seconds

Assessment 4

Date ____________________ Time _______ minutes _______ seconds

Assessment 5 (New guidelines)

Date ____________________ Time _______ minutes _______ seconds

Handwriting: writing quickly but with fluency and legibility. **Grammar:** adjectives (grumpy, quick), classifying adjective (human), common nouns (dancers, volleyballs, taxi, circus), proper noun (Wonthaggi), action verbs (caught, juggle). **Literary elements:** pangram.

Assessment: Progressive self-assessment

Read each of the criteria listed below. When you think you have achieved each one, write the date and sign off.

 My letters are consistently the right shape and an even size. ☐ ____________________

 My letters are a consistent height. ☐ ____________________

 My letters sit on the baseline correctly. ☐ ____________________

 My letter tails hang down correctly. ☐ ____________________

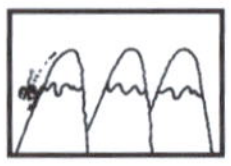 My letters have the same slope. ☐ ____________________

 The space between my letters is regular. ☐ ____________________

 The space between my words is regular. ☐ ____________________

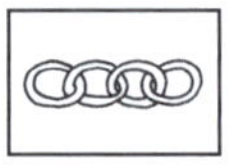 My joins are fluent. ☐ ____________________

 Others can easily read my cursive handwriting. ☐ ____________________

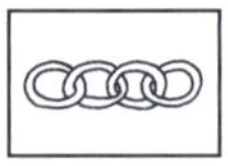 My writing is automatic. (I don't have to think too hard about how to join the letters fluently.) ☐ ____________________

 I can write quickly when I need to and my fast writing is legible to others. ☐ ____________________

 I have started to develop my own personal handwriting style. ☐ ____________________

Have you signed off on each of the criteria?

You've successfully completed your journey to the worlds of FLUENCY and LEGIBILITY.